Made in the USA
Las Vegas, NV
23 May 2025

22599578R10056